M is for Memories

Zuton Lucero-Mills

M is for Memories

Copyright © 2024 by Zuton Lucero-Mills

ISBNs:
978-1944139-42-1 (hardcover)
978-1944139-43-8 (paperback)
978-1944139-44-5 (eBook)

Dedicated to Zumante Malik
August 14, 1999 – July 20, 2009
Mommy loves you.

1

A

A is for *always*. We will *always* remember, and so you will *always* be a part of our lives

A is for *acceptance*.
It is hard to *accept*
that your body is not
here with us, but we
will try to *accept*
that your spirit still
is.

B is for *beauty*. You brought so much to so many.

B

B is for *burden*. The *burden* of your absence is heavy, because we miss your beauty.

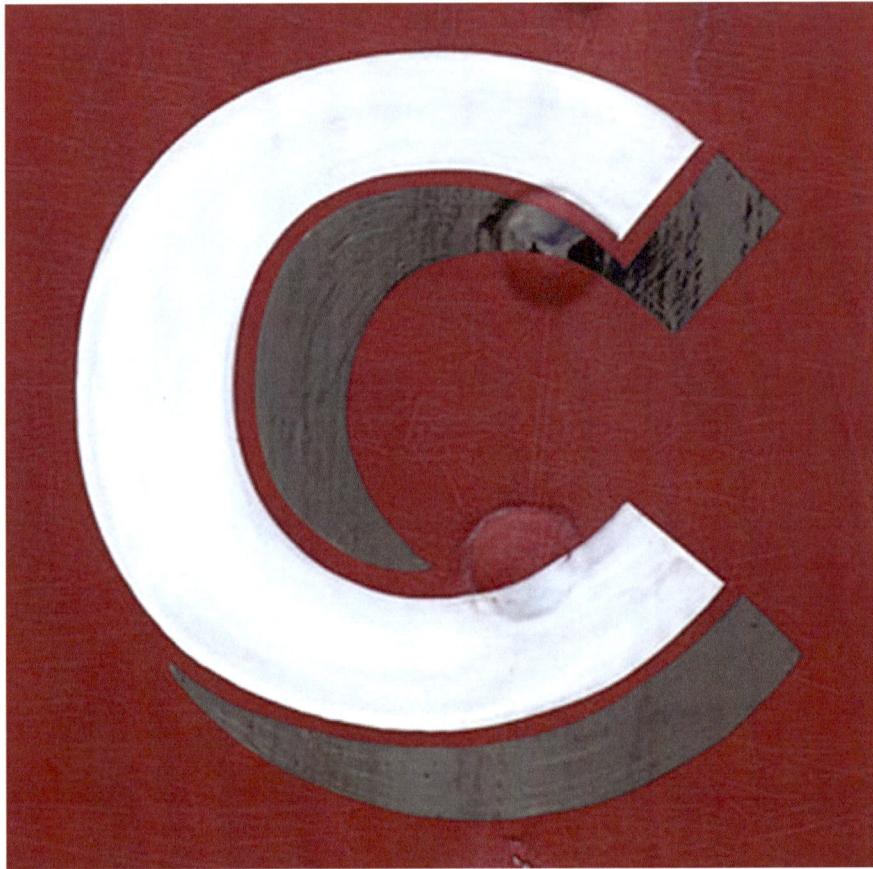

C is for *courage*. You had large *courage*, even as a small person, and we learned from you.

C is for *confusion*. It can be *confusing* when people die, and we wish for some of the courage that you had.

D is for *difference*. It is said that one life makes one. You are proof.

D is for *denial*. We want to *deny* that you are gone. But we can't ignore the difference in our lives.

E is for *example*. All of us have much to learn, but also much to give. You were a very good *example*.

E is for *empty*. Sometimes, this is how things feel without you. We each have to do things in our own way. There is no example for how one has to grieve.

F is for *family*. These are usually the people closest to you. They are the people who love you the hardest. When you are gone, they are the people who carry your memory the closest.

F is for *fear*. When someone you love dies, there is *fear* of how life will continue without them. *Fear* is natural.

G is for *God*. He is all-knowing and all-powerful. He knew how we needed you, and he still decided when to call you home.

G is for *grief*. The dictionary says *grief* is sorrow, anguish, pain, heartbreak, or sadness. I say it is what happened to us when you died.

H is for *heart*. Somehow, a broken one still beats.

H is for
heartbroken.
Heartbreak is an
illness of the
heart. There is no
medicine to buy.

I is for *inspiration*. Your way was not always easy, but you always kept going. We will keep going too.

I is for *interruption*. Your death *interrupted* our lives. It caused us to think about the things that are really important, and what kind of inspiration we should be.

J is for *jewel*. You were a rare gem and we were fortunate to have you shining in our lives.

J is for *judgmental*. Everyone deals with losing a jewel differently. Often, people do not understand one another, and so they *judge* them instead of trying to.

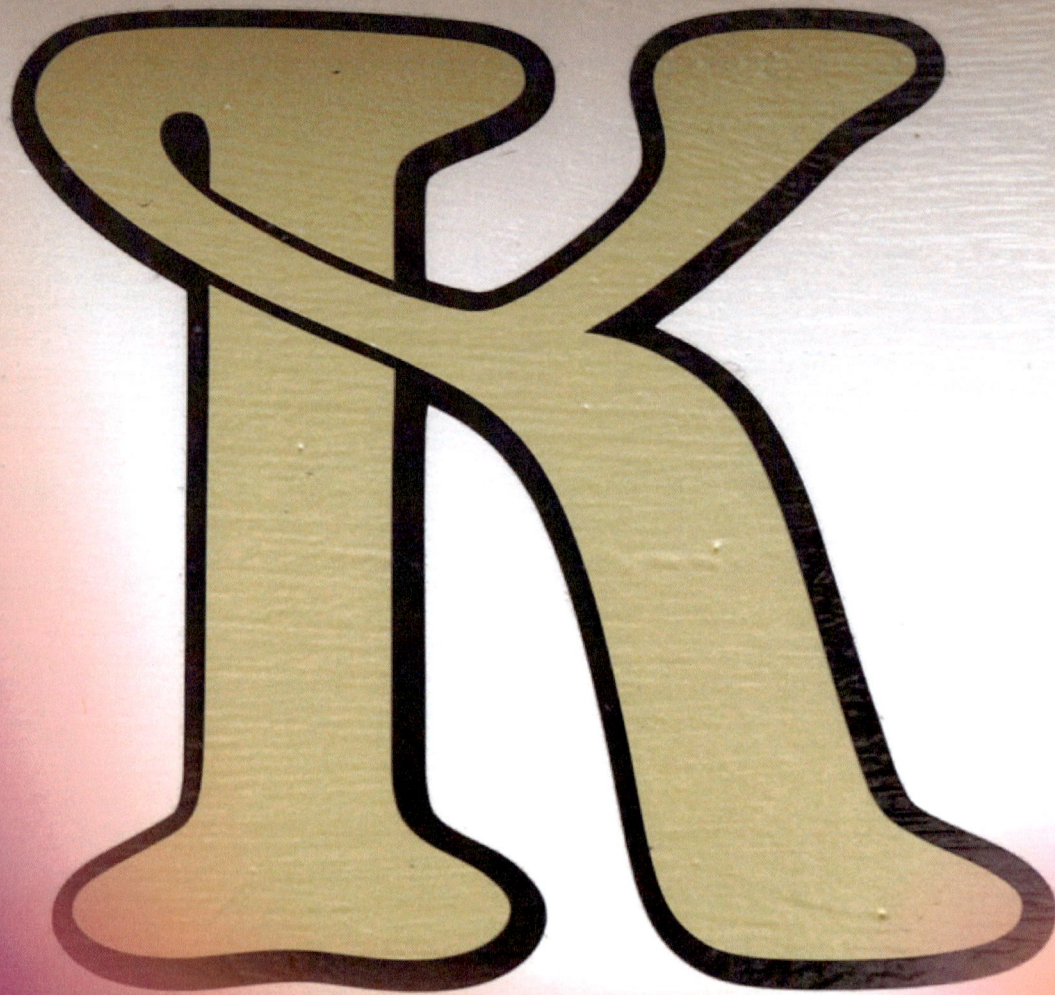

K is for *kindness*. Death rips and shreds the soul. *Kindness* can help to mend it.

K is for *knowledge*. At times, the heart doesn't want to accept death, but the mind *knows* that it is real.

L is for *love*. You were *loved*. You are *loved*. You will be *loved*.

L is for *longing*. We wish you were here. We know you won't be back. We still wish that it was a possibility.

M is for *memories*. Cherished thoughts cover us like cozy, warm blankets. Our *memories* embrace us and we embrace them because it keeps us close to you.

M is for *misery*. *Misery* means suffering. *Misery* means unhappiness. Being *miserable* sometimes is normal.

N is for *necessary*. You brought things into our lives that we never even knew were *necessary*. It is both good and *necessary* that we each leave our own unique handprint on the world.

N is for *nightmares*. They can happen anytime. The scariest *nightmare* is the real one—it is the one where a loved one has died and there is nothing you can do about it.

O is for *opportunity*. When something is not easy, there is an *opportunity* to grow. This is not easy. We are growing.

O is for *outrage*. This is an opportunity we would prefer not to have. We are angry. It is an *outrage* to think of you as dead.

P is for *precious*.
Now that you are
gone, we truly
realize how
precious you were.
You still are.

P is for *pain*. There is *pain* because we want to see you, and speak with you, and hug you. There is *pain* because you have gone ahead, and we have stayed behind.

Q is for *quiet*. *Quiet* can be peaceful and comforting. It can be exactly what a hurting heart needs.

Q is for *questions*. There are always *questions* when a loved one dies. It can be frustrating that we don't have all of the answers.

R is for *reunion*. Someday, we will all be together again. What a joyous *reunion* it will be!

R is for *raw*. The sore is exposed for all to see. It stings. It is not pretty. Some things simply are not.

S is for *strength*. It is important to have people to call on. It is not a sign of weakness to have support. We all need each other.

S is for *sorrow*.
You are gone.
You won't
return
tomorrow.

T is for *time*. We had such an amazing *time* with you. If only the *time* had lasted longer...

T is for *tears*. Many *tears* have been shed. We will cry many more.

U is for *understanding*. We are all here to do good works. Part of those works is taking care of each other.

U is for *unprepared*. We were *unprepared* for the arrival of death. Lots of people are.

V is for *voice*. We must use our *voices* to encourage. The memory of your *voice* still provides encouragement.

V is for *vulnerable*. We are all able to be hurt. Death and grief happen whether you are rich or poor or black or white. In some ways, there are no differences.

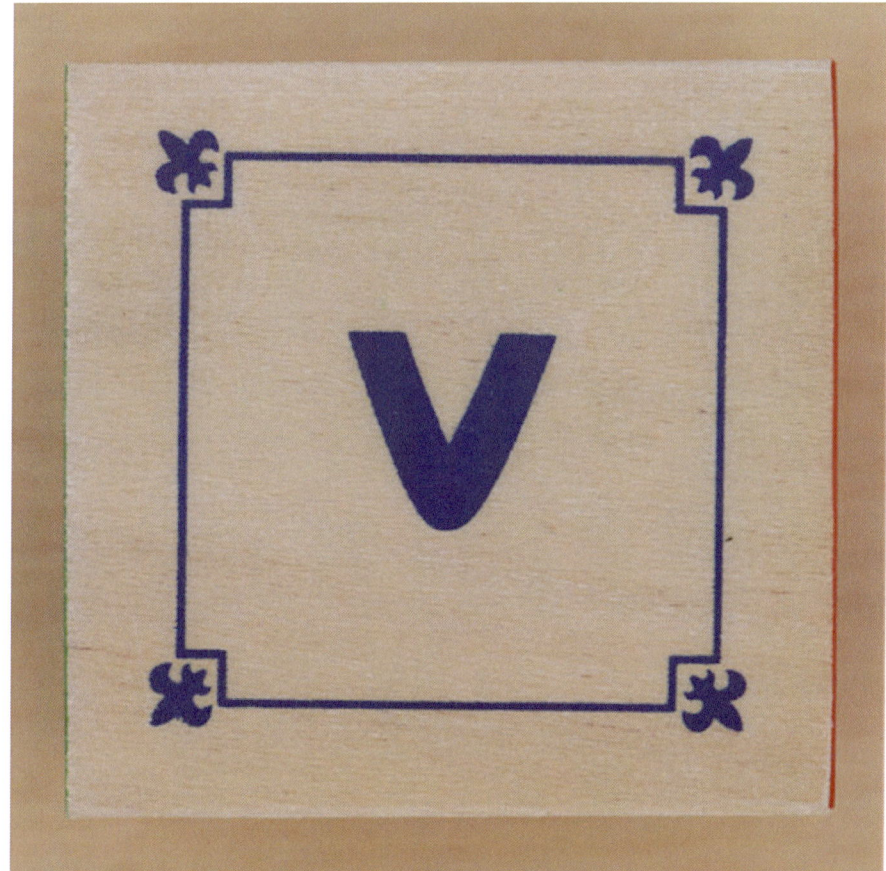

W is for *wonder*. You were a *wonder*. We *wondered* at your level of talent and your ability for love. Everyone should be a *wonder* in some way.

W is for *worry*. Death makes you *worry* about life. It is unpleasant and uncomfortable. It is not uncommon.

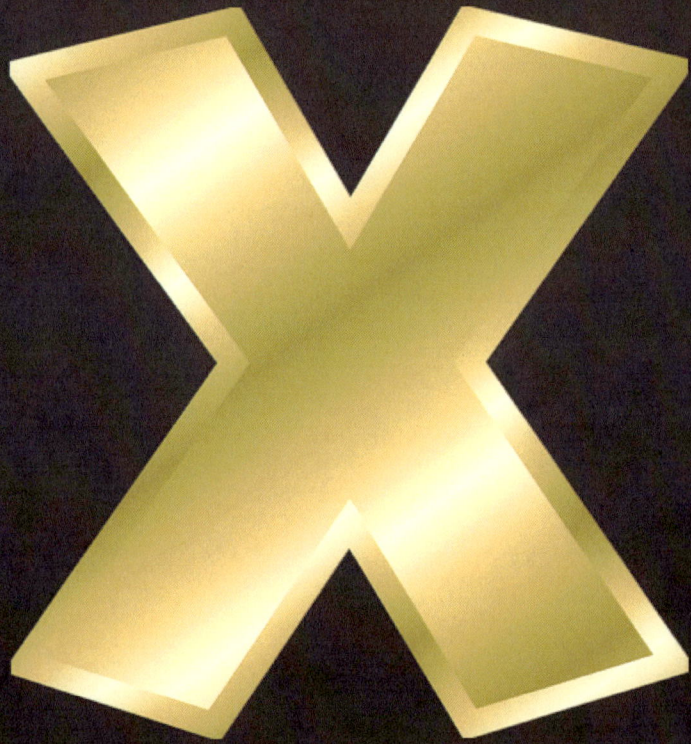

X is for *eXhilarating*. It is good to be excited and cheerful about the business of living. We watched you and learned this lesson. We are practicing.

—

X is for *eXtreme*. Death causes *eXtreme* emotions. There are downs and lower-downs. It makes sense to have big emotions for such a big occurrence.

Y is for *young*. Children lost to death are forever *young*. Those left behind can love like children. It's a good place to start.

Y is for *yearning*. It is a craving. It's a deep desire for something that you don't have. We don't have you.

Z is for Zumante.
In Loving Memory.

About the Author

Zuton Lucero-Mills is a wife and mother. She holds a B.S. in Literary Empowerment for Children and a Master of Social Work degree. Zuton is the editor of *Ten Generations of Bondage: Eleven Generations of Faith*. She has authored three other books, *Mommy's Reflections: Losings Zumante and Finding the Mustard Seed, Higher Than the Heavens and Deeper Than the Grave*, and *Remembering Mimi*. Zuton works as a Grief Counselor and lives in Denver, Colorado with her family.

www.ingramcontent.com/pod-product-compliance
Lightning Source LLC
Chambersburg PA
CBRC100752100426
42813CB00024B/2994